I0163620

Searching for Mozart

Searching for Mozart

Poems

by

Rick Christman

BRIGHT
HORSE
BOOKS

Copyright © 2015 by Rick Christman
All rights reserved.
Printed in the United States of America

Brighthorse Books
13202 N River Drive
Omaha, NE 68112

ISBN: 978-0-9908670-4-3 (paper)
ISBN: 978-0-9908670-5-0 (ebook)

Cover art: istockphoto © Jacques Kloppers

Author photo: Dale Bailey Norris

For permission to reproduce selections from
this book and for more information about
Brighthorse Books and the Brighthorse Prize,
visit us on the web at brighthorsebooks.com.

Contents

Acknowledgments

"Schroeder's Arm" appeared in *Margie*

"War and Shakespeare" appeared in *Oxygen*

"Whiteout: Boondocks, Iowa" appeared in *Wapsipinicon Almanac*

"How War Ruins Hunting" appeared in *Cold Mountain* Review

"Out There Where I Could if I Went" appeared in *Eclipse*

"Returning" appeared in *Happy*

"A Matter of Geography" appeared in *Homestead Review*

"Cabrito, Soldiers, and God" appeared in *The Chariton Review*

"Hanging on at the Blue Danube" appeared in *Wisconsin Review*

"The Pindar of Wakefield" appeared in *Trajectory*

"In a Pig's Eye" appeared in *Wisconsin Review*

"Dreaming" appeared in *Writer to Writer*

"What it Comes Down to" appeared in *Connecticut Review*

"The Real Thing" appeared in *Visions International*

"She Said" appeared in *Oxygen*

"What Remains" appeared in *Connecticut Review*

"P.O.W.'s" appeared in *Poems & Plays*

"Dogs" appeared in *Touchstone*

"Sam Johnson's Gout Chair" appeared in *Rockhurst Review*

"No Escape" appeared in *Stone Canoe*

"Slow Business" appeared in *Steam Ticket*

Colonel A.J. Bailey, Jr., United States Marine
Corps (Retired), and Rupert Christman,
United States Army Air Corps

To the love of my life,
Dale Bailey Norris.
Without her, this book
would never have been written.

Searching for Mozart

Schroeder's Arm

I saw his armless sleeve flap in a strong breeze
In Beaufort, South Carolina,
Flap open like a mouth,
Flap closed like a wave goodbye.
And I thought how he must be making a statement,
This guy–
No prosthesis,
Just an empty sleeve.
See, he must be saying:
I lost my arm in the war,
Blown off my shoulder
Like a twig in a strong wind.
The other day
Someone even called me a one-armed-son-of-a-bitch.
But I remember when I had two,
Like you.
I called Cadence across the Bay at Parris Island,
Both of my arms firm,
Swinging to the rhythm of my future.

But now I stand in the middle of my room,
Drink scotch late at night,
Try to remember
Pain in this empty sleeve–
The bump and sting of a playful punch,
The dull ache of throwing a ball too hard, too long,
The thump, thump, thump of a rifle butt.
I wait for things to happen,
Like everyone waits for things to happen,
For my sleeve to fill up again,
Hard, permanent this time,
Like molten steel poured to harden into a mold.

Searching for Mozart

Someone once told me that
Mozart could change my life.
So I bought a ticket for Salzburg,
Even though the battles still raged in my mind,
Stiffening my spine
And clouding my vision like a veil.

The train had once been
The Orient Express – I saw a faded sign
Stamped in white on one of the cars.
But my car bucked and banged and rocked on the track
Like a cattle car,
The lights flickering on and off
Until they flickered off for good.
I sat in the dark the rest of the way,
Like an animal, listening,
Waiting to be taken to a midnight slaughter.

But in the morning,
When the doors opened,
The world exploded like a new beginning,
And I spent hours scanning the Alps
That surrounded me,
Searching like a blind man
Whose sight has suddenly been restored,
Searching for what had inspired Mozart.

In the afternoon,
I drank beer with three new Austrian friends
From glass steins so large
I could barely lift them with two hands.
The Austrians shook their fingers at me from all sides,

Like Sunday school teachers
Instructing a wayward boy.
Mozart's music was a gift from God, they said.
I needed to listen to Elvira Madigan,
Allow every note to become part of me.
Mozart would cleanse my soul
Like a waterfall falling through me
From the high mountains that surrounded us.

I knew they were right.
And Mozart and the Alps
Were just what I needed.
But I also knew
The war clutched at me every minute,
Like a vice-grip on my heart,
Refusing to leave me at peace,
And I had more trips to come,
Many dark and alone,
Like the train car that had brought me to Salzburg.

Nothing Else but Words

My tenth grade English teacher saved my life
When she forced me to memorize poems.
Shakespeare, Dickinson, Frost, and especially Whitman,
Spilled over everything in that northern Wisconsin class-
    room.
I volunteered to recite every chance I got.
As I stood in front of the class,
Floating from foot to foot,
Words swam through my mind.
"I celebrate myself and sing myself."
Words burst from my mouth
Like water through a garden hose.

At home, words continued to flow through me
Like the Black River waters that played
Over the rocks outside my open bedroom window.
As I watched and listened at midnight
To the dark, rushing waters,
I heard the river speak to me.
As I lay in my bed,
The river sang the poems I memorized:
"Out of the cradle endlessly rocking . . .
Out of the ninth month midnight,"
As if the river gave the words reality
Outside my open window,
Outside my saturated mind.

Later, I recited quietly as we lay in ambush.
I let the words spill over me,
Hoping they would protect me like armor.
Once the flares lit the sky like bonfires and the firing began,
I buried my face in the rank mud and recited.

"And what I shall assume, you shall assume,
For every atom belonging to me as good belongs to you."
While others died around me,
The repetition of sounds filled my mind
And nothing pierced the shield of my words
Until there was nothing else but words,
Until the firing stopped for good
And there was only the smell of cordite
And the smell of dying men.

Cello Dreams

She played the cello to me over the phone,
Someone's younger sister.
I imagined a black phone on a black table,
White notes rising off her cello,
Beethoven's Seventh,
Because I'd told her it was my favorite,
Though I didn't know Beethoven from Bach
In those days.
And the war still had its hooks in me.

The calls came in the middle of the night,
Jerking me out of my nightmares,
My world of mortars and ambushes,
Explosions stark and wrenching,
My imagination pulling me back
To the past.

The calls continued,
Night after night.
Month after month.
Her cello began soothing the war out of me
As I discovered only music can,
The Magic Flute and The Swan
Began to wipe those nightmares away
Like a clean cloth wipes away dirty water.

Until I dreamed in music.
I lay in my bed, waiting and listening
For cello dreams,
A nineteenth-century orchestra,
Fur Elise, Moonlight Sonata, Elvira Madigan,
Cello bows moving like hummingbirds

Over the strings,
Filling the hall with music,
Lifting me up,
Until I dreamed a future.

War and Shakespeare

Paging old poetry books
Like a despaired priest
Still in search of a halo,
I saw your name again.
And I remembered how
The night was real,
And the world rocked and shook
With other men's dreams,
While we huddled in a bunker
Like rats in a sewer,
And read your love sonnets
By flashlight.

Whiteout: Boondocks, Iowa

The cold saps the world of breath, and the snow surrounds us, closes in. We have come to this place, this truck stop in central Iowa off Interstate 35, huddled together in two small rooms, gathered like prisoners, forced off the highway to become more than we are.

We gather chairs and stools into a tight ring and smoke. One of the drivers relates casually losing his truck, panic stricken, on harrowing mountain roads. Once you're committed, he says, you have to go through with it. You have no choice. You ever hear a truck go by—*whoosh*—you know? He grins and drops his eyes, then opens them wide suddenly and stares at us, from one to the other. We scrape our chairs, our stools, closer.

Another driver, one without long underwear peeking through his shirt front, without even a tee shirt, circulates, refuses to join us. As he paces the room, he relates loudly the intimate details of his life. He punches holes into the air with his cigarette fist. The heat in here is enough to suffocate you, he says again and again. Damn it, don't they know there is never enough cool air?

A blonde, high-school-aged waitress rushes through the room, the hem of her tan and brown checked uniform rising and falling, rising and falling, like hours passing: twelve, twenty-four, thirty-six. Food is running out in the restaurant, she shouts to us, to the cashier across the room, to anyone who will listen. Her eyes, too, are wide, large, light brown, but she turns quickly away from us and heads back into the restaurant. Food is running out, she calls one last time on her way out.

A man who looks like Hemingway comes in out of the night, his full gray beard frozen like crystal. He walks directly to the corner of the room and stares at the brown wall and talks. My God, he says. He has just come in off the road. The snow swirled around his lost vehicle for two hours, and now all he can do is look at the dark wall and talk. He was driving straight into the air, he says. And the white. So *white* everywhere. Before he joins us, he touches the wall, finally, the brown, his fingers caressing it like it is skin.

There are even blacks here in central Iowa, in off the road from Des Moines, on the way to St. Paul and Minneapolis. They cluster together among this Midwestern prairie white, in the midst of all this incredible white snow. They move together about the filled rooms, caroming enclaves of black. But as the hours pass, they stop moving about and look from one to the other. They grab chairs and stools and slide easily into the circle, into the spaces we provide for them.

Cigarette-fist-man crowds in among us, too, finally, and admits, whispers softly, his breath, his words almost visible, how in Vietnam helicopter blades swirled the jungle, vibrated the jungle, moved the grass like snow on his feet, his legs, to his waist. It was like life there, he says, but it was the heat, waves of substantial air trapping his breath in his throat. And now, since, he can't get cool enough. He will never again be cool enough. He strips his shirt then, there in front of us, to his naked, sweat-beaded skin. Cool, he says, and then tells about actually punching holes into the walls of his house for cool, cool air. As he talks, we hear sounds in the night, snow sanding the windows, tapping like fingers, as it swirls around us, then over toward 35.

But the wind and the snow die suddenly, as if they had never been. At once we rise and step lightly, nearly jaunting, out to our vehicles, as if nothing ever happened, as if the world remained the same the whole time. The drivers move on to their jobs without thinking, blowing down mountain roads whoosh. And the blacks move back into the white world.

I wait, lag behind, then head to my own vehicle, alone, last, after all are gone. Half way there I stop and feel the world, dark as death out in the night. And it cracks suddenly—I can hear it crack—splits us apart, hard, complete, sundered, like logs beneath the axe.

How War Ruins Hunting

Dawn and into the dark, lowland woods—
It's damp as a jungle in there.
I see them right away,
Shadows, then two bucks, two does,
Snorting, their breath like smoke about their noses,
Standing abreast, like men in ranks,
Waiting.
I close my eyes and see them moving at port arms,
Coming toward us.
And we each have death
In the palms of our hands.

I run, run,
Three miles up the hill to high timber, blue sky,
A place like no other.
I gulp clear cold air, hold it, gulp more.
And I know only one thing:
War ruins hunting.

How a River Becomes Just a River

I returned to my northern Wisconsin home
And the beloved Black River of my youth.
The river still rushed by my bedroom window at midnight.
The water still moved like a black ribbon
On and on to the end and back.
But the river no longer spoke poetry to me as it once had.
Instead, the black waters stirred deep and empty.
They reeked of dead fish
And they threatened to pull me down
Into their dark wordless movement.
So I kept my distance.
I knew that the river had become just a river.

Out There Where I Could if I Went

I had never been much for nature.
The smell of damp leaves and rushing spring water,
Surrounded by pine forests that closed in,
Clung close to my ears like mosquitoes,
Pushed foot-heavy on my chest.

No, I stayed in,
Smelled root beer and bubblegum,
Drove quiet town streets,
Felt the swirl of prom dresses,
Tasted the sting of real beer.

I spurned my friends' invitations to hunt and to fish,
Watched them head out on foot
In thick brown boots
And blue and red plaid shirts.

Out there.
Where I could if I went.

Push brush aside with my bare hands,
Breathe deep, cold, Black River waters,
Thrust my hands to the bottom,
Splash my face clean.

I kept clear of all of that.
Until the war pushed me in deep,
Forced the hot, wet jungle,
Held me down,
Slammed my face hard
Into snakes and fungal smells.

Out there.
Where I could if I went.

All the Way to the Bottom

I wish I still fished like I did when I was ten,
Long before the war and all that came later.
I'd wait for my uncle to arrive from the city
In the middle of the night in the spring.
We'd head off in his car together at dawn,
My uncle wearing his jaunty city hat,

Just the two of us,
The sun burning off the cold mist
Over the dark Wisconsin forests
Like a new beginning.

We'd find an empty shore on the Yellow or the Black,
Or a boat where we didn't need a motor,
One I could row out myself,
As if I weren't skinny and ten
But a man with arms like Popeye's.

Once we found our spot,
We'd sit,
Silent together over the flat blue empty water,
Until I reached into the cold,
Felt the water's presence living in my hand.
And we could both see
All the way to the bottom.

What if My Life is a Comic Strip?

I was born late.
I even started school late,
A momma's boy wandering the foreign halls,
Lost and alone,
The smell of chalk and the sweat of others
In my nose,
Unable to read, unable to write.

I went to the war late.
I ran late for the last bunker,
Just as everything inside exploded into my face
In blood and pieces.
Then I returned home late,
The last one off the last plane,
Like an afterthought.

I fell in love late.
I searched for love day and night,
Like a blind pigeon searches for food.
And now when my head is gray,
As Chekhov says,
And it's too late,
I've fallen in love properly.

But then, I think,
What if irony hits me over my gray head
Like a tap from a soft baton,
And I die . . . early?
What if my life is a comic strip
Starring a bumbling guy who's always late,
But who dies early?

Not long before he died,
My father looked at me
From an old man's sagging cheeks,
Dementia graying his blue eyes,
And said: "I thought you knew better than that."
But I've never known better than that.
Because I've always been late.

Returning

The five of them had been so young, and had spent so little time learning the ropes in America before they left for the war, that they had never learned the knack of making money. And since the blaring horns, back-firing cars, and sharp, loud voices of even small village streets banged horribly on their sensitive ears, like artillery, like the rat-tat-tat of machine gun fire and the screams of dying men, they made a pact: once they were out of the war and out of the army for good, they would disappear into the wilderness together forever. So three days after they were finally processed out once and for all, they built a one-room cabin ten miles from the Lac Du Flambeau Reservation, deep in the huge Chequamegon Forest in Northern Wisconsin.

In the summertime, the men stripped off their shirts and fished barefoot all day long together on the same stream bank, though on different rocks, far enough away from each other to provide a necessary, unspoken space. In winter, they fished through small, perfectly spaced holes hacked into the ice, or they strung thin, looped wire along rabbit runways and snared their simple meals. Sometimes they even picked wild blackberries from a small patch half a mile from their cabin to add to their meat. Then later, every evening, the five of them huddled together silently and drank hootch from the still they tended behind the cabin. They drank on into the late night. They drank until their eyes finally drooped and their bottles slipped from their hands. Eventually they stretched out onto their beds and slept until late morning, dreaming the war away. Until they rose to begin again.

* * *

On the twentieth of July, five days after zinc had been discovered in the Chequamegon Forest, Exxon began preparing the pit mine. A two-hundred-man crew with chainsaws looped into their belts and with machetes the size of ancient battle axes in their powerful hands headed into the forest, while others in giant cowboy hats guided bulldozer blades and deep mouth shovels behind them. They cut, smashed, bulldozed and flattened. Then they scraped and they chopped and they dug. The crew moved non-stop through the forest, grinding and flattening and digging, a thing alive and inevitable, like a herd of marauding dinosaurs. They went at it all day long, until the sun sank low enough in the sky to darken the thick forest. Then the next morning they went at it again.

* * *

When the five men heard the crew coming, the noise rising and falling, louder and louder, chewing and roaring and shaking the earth, they knew the world had to be ending. So they did the only thing they could do. They left everything behind and ran as they were, shirtless and barefoot, wide-eyed and deranged, like all who know the end is near. As they heard the crew reach their cabin behind them, they ran together, side by side, brushing by trees and leaping fallen logs. By the time the cabin had been flattened and buried in the black earth beneath, like it had never been there at all, they were nearly a mile away. They continued to run until their sides ached, until they were forced to stop briefly and vomit into the brush before moving on again. They ran and they ran and they ran. And then they ran some more.

Eventually, their breath gave out, and they began to trip and to fall. They rolled onto the ground again and again, held their stomachs and groaned. But each time, something profound and mysterious within picked them up and pushed them on, anyway, long after they should have been finished.

Finally, however, when the five men could rise up no longer, even for a brief moment, they gave up entirely, lay down

34

forever and let the earth do what it would with them. And they died together, spread out on the ground head to head in a perfect ring, like ancient Aborigines who had broken the pole of life.

A Matter of Geography

After I returned from the war
I thought I'd seen everything.
But then, Erie County Jail and a con down from Attica,
An ex-biker called Running Bear,
Is talking, strutting,
Scraggily-assed hair,
Deep black eyes no one dares look into.
He'd take a contract out on anybody
For Five G's.
Everybody in the block is nodding,
Black, white,
Yeah, damn straight,
Close in,
Close enough to smell each other's stink,
To suck in each other's breath.
And Running Bear turns to me,
Laughs a killer laugh,
Eyeteeth filed to Devil's points,
Says killing's all a matter of Geography, man,
All a matter of Geography.

Sam Johnson's Gout Chair

Because my wife and I wanted to sit where Johnson sat,
Imagine what he imagined,
Feel his Circle tighten around us,
And because the war still trailed after me,
We settled in at the Cheshire Cheese late that morning.
We ordered slabs of lamb and roast beef
Like size twelve shoes.
Then, later, we headed around the alley
To his house in Gough Square.

The ancient caretaker was still in her bonnet when we arrived.
She talked solemnly of the great man,
Her voice like a dove's.
Dr. Johnson, Dr. Johnson, she cooed,
As if she might break apart at any moment from the strain,
As if she had loved him and still did,
As if he had died the day before.

Then I spotted his gout chair,
So fragile now,
Like a child's chair.
My wife headed over
But the caretaker shooed me away
When I neared Johnson's seat of humiliation.
So while my wife sat,
I stood back and imagined Johnson,
Sitting all those years ago,
Like a mountain falling,
Groaning into the sea,
Alone.

I wanted to imagine more of Johnson's life
In that house,
In that chair,
To stay there for hours and
Soothe the war out of my soul with the past.
But we pulled ourselves away instead,
Like friends parting for the last time,
As the caretaker waved her tiny bird hand
Through the narrow front window.

Cabrito, Soldiers, and God

The day we both returned
From the war
We drove to Monterey in an old red Dodge with fins
That rocked like a boat
And made us both feel like explorers
Heading out onto the brown desert, into the hot sun.

In the city, we watched butchers in white coats
Chop hot roasted cabrito,
Bones and all,
With large, honed, chopping knives, like machetes,
Meat, kid goat, we thought,
Barely alive,
And dump it into white boxes for dinner.

Later, as we headed into the mountains,
Young Mexican militia stopped us
On the side of the road,
Pointed, waved M-16's at us
Like toy guns.
We stood with our hands spread on the car,
Our backs hunched like old soldiers,
Waiting for the firing to begin.
But they only wanted to see inside
Our empty trunk.

In Taxco, we drank small bottles of Carta Blanca beer
From the balcony on Christmas Eve,
Toasted our good fortune again and again,
Watched the procession of virgin girls
Carry candles—the flames barely flickering—
Leading the way further up the mountain

To God.

On the way back to Laredo
I stopped the car
And we walked over to a village well,
Pumped the old handle until cold, clean water poured
Over our hands, over our heads, over our faces,
A cleansing,
For better or for worse.

Hanging on at the Blue Danube

That summer,
I waited an hour at Schmidt's in Vienna to eat Weiner
    Schnitzel
The size of garbage can lids.
Later I drank sweet Trappist beer with two local couples
Who invited me along to the dance.
So I shouted my best German
And stomped my feet like a Dukhobor,
Drank schnapps until I stumbled out lost
Onto the empty streets at midnight.

But I wanted to see the Blue Danube
Like I'd imagined the first time I'd heard Strauss's waltz.
The water out the bay windows
As blue as the sky turns at dusk,
While lords and ladies danced the gilded halls.

So I found my way to the river and hung onto the bridge,
Like a child staring down at water for the first time.
The Danube looked as blue as my fantasy in the evening,
Under the skylights,
Though I knew that in the harsh daylight
The water would be as deep brown as caramel sludge,
And would carry McDonald's wrappers and Budweiser
    bottles
Out of the ancient city into the Austrian countryside.

Yeats and Billy O'Connor

I stand before Yeats' grave,
The simple sandstone marker,
The humpbacked hill in the distance,
And remember Billy O'Connor.
I imagine Billy's South Boston elementary classroom,
His swaying, gray-haired teacher,
Hands on his lapels as if he were holding himself up,
Reciting before giggling white-faced boys:
"I will arise and go now."

I remember Billy standing before me in our bunker,
His pale face and his dark eyes
Illuminated by a flare,
Grasping his collar like lapels,
His voice clear,
The voice of home—
"I will arise and go now."

I remember the mortar that hit Billy dead on
As he headed out into the night,
Like an arrow to his heart,
Shooting fire into the sky,
His one, true, passionate moment.

The Pindar of Wakefield

I remember Johnny Joe Watson
Instructing me on Marx
As we ducked for our lives in Bong Song,
His eyes lit like Marx's must have been,
Burning into me.
The proletariat, Johnny cried,
The Bourgeoisie.
Dreaming all of us equal
And forever in the throes of right.

The next fall,
I walked five miles down Old Brompton Road
To the Pindar of Wakefield,
The exact spot where Marx
Plotted the fall of Capitalism,
His beard pointing the way toward
The future.

But by the time I arrived
The place had forgotten Marx,
Jazz on Friday,
Rock on Saturday,
Two for one Wednesday nights.
Though it still had the stink of the working class,
Diesel fuel, cigarette smoke, piss and beer
Floating over everyone.

Smoke

In the early morning at the Eyre Hotel in Galway,
A hungover waiter in a rumpled white shirt and black tie,
Smelling of stale beer and tobacco,
Serves me an empty blue china coffee pot
With my full Irish breakfast.

Later in the morning,
Old men smoking,
Fishing for salmon with cane poles
Along the Corrib,
A winding river that cuts like a blade
Through the center of the old city,
The men's cigarettes pointing west
Like sign markers
Toward the Bay.

In the afternoon along the blue Bay water,
"No littering, no butts on the beach,"
Men walk by in pairs,
Smoking,
Their cigarettes incandescent sticks,
Like defiant candles of freedom.

In the evening,
Pints at a pub along the docks.
The sting of smoke in my eyes,
In my hair.
"You can't get throat cancer
If you don't smoke 'em."

I buy a pack of Pall Mall reds,
Light up,

Fill my lungs to never release them,
Smoke into the night,
Into the end,
A man on a mission,
A man filled with smoke.

No Escape

From a safe distance,
I watch teenage Mexican boys on Plaza Garibaldi,
Stripped to bare feet and jeans,
Swallow fire at midnight.
Fire shoots from their mouths
Like bottle rockets
Down the row of boys,
One after another,
Into the night sky.

The smell of gasoline
Takes my breath,
Like the boys take fire.
I rush away, escape the burning
Toward the horns and yodels of Mariachis.
I find a booth among the throng
And slide in alone.

But at once men surround me,
Push into my booth from both sides,
Trap me like a rabbit in a wire snare,
Until I know that there will be no escape.
They buy me a cold Carta Blanca
But they feed me fire,
Birria red sauce spilling over my tacos—
I can see the flames.
I switch to green sauce
But I find no relief from fire.

Later that night,
Alone
From the balcony of my hotel,

I watch fire shoot into the Mexican sky and die,
Shoot and die,
Like night fighting, I think,
And I wait to hear the explosions,
But I know it's only fireworks.
A little later, still,
I think of Tommy Sojourner,
Trapped alone,
On fire in his jeep,
And not one of us could save him.

Slow Business

I was planted like a weed in a drab Right Bank café.
The only French I knew
Was for ordinary red wine and draft beer,
Vin vang ordinaire, biere du pression.
So that's what I drank,
Two rounds of each,
Until the whores arrived.

They landed anywhere the night took them,
Like painted birds,
Red and yellow dresses off their smooth shoulders,
Hems hiked to their laps.
Their harsh voices revved up the quiet café at midnight.
They were good customers
So the waiter in a dingy white shirt hustled
From zinc bar to table and back,
His shoes sliding like he was on ice.

I knew the whores were as bored as
The empty night air
And that they wanted the world to hear, to know.
And I was sure, too,
Even with the war still at my back closing fast
And so little French,
That business was slow
In a profession they say never goes out of style.

On Seeing Charlemagne's Throne

I remember Charlemagne's beard
From pictures in grade school history books,
Hanging all the way to his knees like a braided rug.
The Leader of the Known World,
His sword taller than he was,
Still dripping the blood of his enemies.

But now, in Achean,
His empty wood throne
Stands behind a simple rope cordon.
I have just returned from my own battles,
But I have no bloody sword at my side,
No distant lands to conquer.

In A Pig's Eye

In A Pig's Eye, the place was called,
Somewhere in South London,
Near Brixton—I'd heard about the riots, the fires.
And the war still clung to me.
So I looked for a Catholic Church,
A late Saturday afternoon mass.
I saw a cross on the map
Like a tiny white finger, pointing—St. Anne's.

Lost, I ended up here.
Someone's local.
No place for tourists.
I'd been panhandled on the way in
By a bearded man
In a faded orange and white checked shirt,
Like a rag of freedom.

I huddled at a table in a dark corner,
Sipped small glasses of beer.
Smoke and the smell of piss
From the corner toilet door covered everything,
Rough black and brown men
Glowered,
Slammed dice and gulped pints,
Foam on their lips, their chins,
Like they couldn't get the stuff down fast enough,
As the sun dropped below the horizon
Out the only window.

Anne Frank's House

I came to Amsterdam to cleanse myself in the Old World,
Along the canals, the Brown Cafés,
Among ancient men drinking lemon flavored gin,
Their Dutch voices gruff with experience,
Stuffing pipes, talking of the great wars.

I wanted to talk, too,
To say that I'd seen the enemy up close,
Stabbed with bayonets,
Lifted off of their feet into the air,
Like empty clothes.

Later, I stood in front of Anne Frank's house.
I had read the Diary as a boy.
Anne Frank, a young dark-haired girl trembling behind a wall
In the dark,
High topped black boots
Clicking the pavement, searching,
As the war rushed over everyone
Like a storm the house couldn't hold.
But I didn't go in.

Finally, everything passed,
Like it always does,
In the Anne Frank Pub down the street,
Surrounded by young people who didn't care,
And who only used the toilet
Hidden behind a poster-covered wall
To amuse the customers.

To Whatever Came Next

That first winter,
We could no longer stand the Wisconsin cold,
So we drove my orange Volkswagen Bug down Route 66
With the Beatles and the Rolling Stones,
On the road in search of America,
Like Buzz and Tod(d) in that early sixties TV show—
Except their hair was short
And they drove a blue Corvette—
The brown desert sands
And the blue, open, treeless spaces
Stretching into a future with nothing but the pain
That comes from the emptiness of lost love.

But then rumbling and flashing
Attacked us on the horizon,
Fiery streaks striking across a dark sky.
I looked at you in your three-day growth
And you nodded slowly
But your eyes screamed Yes!
And I hit the brakes hard
And we spun and dove into the desert sands for cover,
Amazed that after all we'd been through in the jungle
Our time had finally come,
Out in this barren place
Without even a single tree.
And so we lay on our bellies
Like the snakes that must have been all around us,
Seething and closing in from the rear,
While we waited for the mortars and the rockets
To attack us from the front.

But then, an hour later,
After the rumbling and the flashing melted
Into the deep blue of the sky
And we were sure,
Without any idea why,
That this attack had spared us
And had moved on over the gold and white mountains
In the distance to the northeast,
We could continue on our journey.

War Crimes

I went to Brussels to discover the truth
About war crimes.
I thought I'd seen a few.
But all I discovered in Brussels
Were serious old men in robes
Sitting like babies in highchairs,
A stage filled with dancing puppets,
A peeing stone manikin,
And *moules a la marinere* and beer
In a café called Death.

Dreaming

After Vietnam, Beck lived alone for thirty years—he never married, never fathered a child, never even dreamed. He suppressed his war years, tight, hidden, like a stone he had swallowed and his body never released. He had done like his father before him had done, after WW II, gone to work to build the community. Like father like son, Beck thought, both wrapped tight, like mummies, decayed, wrapped for good. But suddenly, after thirty years, he began dreaming, and he dreamed night after night. The dreams slipped into his bedroom like intruders, uninvited, and grasped him, held him high, as if to inspect him, twisted him this way and that, prodded him to confess. Night after night. And it was the same dream, beginning to end.

Three of them, Erickson, Hanlon and Williams stepped forward, one after the other, the details stark, their faces bright and firm and well-defined; the dream pervaded with vibrancy, beauty and youth, even in the dark tragedy of their blood-soaked, sweat-spattered uniforms. Each took his turn, spoke to him, accused him. He had lived and they had died, inhabiting only his dreams.

And why him? They had all four gone to Vietnamese language school together in Washington D.C. So why Beck? Why had he survived? All their training the same, the same friends, speaking the strange Asian words, repeating like ducks quacking, *Ong di dau, Ong di ve nha*, up and down, a strange tonal reality of its own, over and over, the four of them careening drunk down crowded Washington streets in Hanlon's chipped blue Volkswagen Bug, no tomorrow, nothing but that stretched silver moment, laughing like friends forever.

Erickson, nineteen, blond, paunchy, the smile of God's innocent, Purdue at sixteen, stubborn, believing in the right

thing—"Beck," he'd say, adamant, his sweet blue eyes search-
ing for approval, "those people over there in Asia need us,"
later, near the end of language school, carrying on a love
affair with their eighteen year old teacher, Co The, before the
eyes of everyone, the brass, school officials—assigned to the
1st Infantry, the Big Red One, two months later a perfectly
spaced sniper's bullet through his stubborn forehead on a
Ben Cat bunker. And now Erickson was gone forever, only a
dream. And Beck had lived.

Hanlon, red haired and freckled, from the fringes of
Okefenokee—he'd know plenty about "jungles and such,"
when the four of them got to the war. His tan and pale blue
seersucker suits flared out behind him as they walked the
corridors together in language school, broad sun-tanned face,
"gators and snakes," he'd said, forcing a smile, "and quick bites
to the death"—twenty-three, old for the draft, but after Flor-
ida Presbyterian College, there had been nothing left but to
let the Army suck him up with the rest, and after basic train-
ing, his father's puffed Southern pride seeing him for the first
time in his uniform—"man, what could I do *then*?"—Hanlon,
smoking his Pall Mall straights down to the tip—they all four
smoked everything down to the tip—attached to the 101st
Airborne, forced to drop from airplanes, fly, legs spread like a
red scarecrow, shot out of his Bien-Hoa jeep during Tet, ten
AK rounds up and down his linguist's back like an exclama-
tion mark. Hanlon. He was dead. And Beck had lived.

And Williams—tall, hard, strong Williams, Kansas State
linebacker kicked out of school for screwing the wrong local
white girl, drafted two days later—"man, they call that ug-
ly-ass town *Manhattan*"—a gift for language, for sounds,
tones, nuances, even—"you three white boys a little too pale
to be real"—Williams with his gifts, his generous nature—he

sent all but fifty dollars every month back to Brooklyn to help his mother and little sister—assigned to the 1st Air Cav, the *Cav*, who hated linguists, sent him swooping down in helicopters, dragging the wounded from the ground to the sky, day after day, one mission after another, shot down, captured, tortured, starved for two years, like a dried and burned black stick when they found him in a dry river bed a hundred miles from where he began. So Williams was dead and Beck had lived. They had all died and here he remained, alive, untouched.

* * *

Beck awakens now, shaken, his dream over. He feels the pungi stakes that he has only heard about piercing his chest, the sharpened sticks entering deeply, painfully. He rises, walks to his bedroom window and looks out at the black sky, stars, the full moon, a man looking down at him from the white surface that he has never before been able to see. He walks the floor, beats his chest with his fist, driving the stakes deeper, his lips anemic, turned to dried apples, his eyes to pale blue china plates. He feels the cold hardwood floor on his bare feet, shivers break out on the backs of his arms, his legs, down to the tip of his spine. He blinks as he walks, waits for revelation. He thinks about killing himself, thinks hard, like sinking underground into the black wet suffocating earth. But instead he paces night after night, waiting for the next dream, his duty now, dreaming them alive, living with their deaths like the black granite Wall in the center of his heart.

What It Comes Down To

Your daughters are disposing of your life
In brown cardboard boxes
From the grocery store down the street.
I hear their lively voices in the next room.
I imagine one of them
Inspecting some memento
Held out on her fingertips,
Before tossing it into the discarded pile.

Your Zippo, maybe, I think,
The one you carried from Okinawa to Chosin,
Like your personal cross,
The one you well could have prayed to,
Dented by shrapnel into a perfect round hole
Where a pea could have fit.

Or even your best friend's worn rabbit's foot,
Your wingman who disappeared one afternoon,
Fire spiraling downward
Like an arrow had been shot into the sky,
The arc, then the descent.
Gone.
So quickly you weren't even sure
You'd seen it happen,
Until that night his rabbit's foot lay
Forgotten on his pillow.

Or your dog tags,
Clutched in your right hand
For the ultimate good luck
As you bobbed like a sofa on the empty sea,
Your blue Corsair floating,

Sinking around you piece by piece like a child's toy,
Signaling the end.

And now,
As I hear their voices in the next room,
 I remember seeing you for the final time,
Alone,
The smell of age on your shoulders,
Your bony arms between your knees
Like dry sticks,
Waiting for someone
To put food into your mouth.

Wars Become Stories

On the first anniversary of your death,
I walk out there in the shadows,
Like someone about to break in.
Others live in your house now,
In the midst of their own stories.
But I want to see the porch again
Where we sat together that night,
Smell the smoke rising from your cigar
With every word you spoke,
Your fingers pinching the ivory Philippine cigar holder,
Drinking cognac as if it might run out
Before all of the stories were told—
Revealed—
Made real again one last time.

"Wars become stories in the end—
That's all that's left when everyone is gone."
Your damaged Corsair
Catching only its front wheels onto the carrier,
Rocking on the edge but holding.
"Like a man who can't swim
Holding onto the edge of a swimming pool
In deep water."
Just long enough to pull you out
Before your plane dropped into the sea.

The night before you returned from Korea,
Your plane flipping on the runway
And you hanging suspended in your harness,
The harness designed to save you,
Fuel dripping over you
Like a low pressure shower.

You held your breath for the end,
The spark that never came.

I see myself now,
Sitting beside you
That last summer night,
The cognac bottle empty,
Your cigar stubbed out.
I remember wanting
To say something moving,
Something profound,
Until you rose, finally,
And limped back inside for the last time.

The Real Thing

If I could only hear my father's voice one last time
Scratch gruff over the telephone like Scarlet Fever,
Listen to him tell about Prohibition
When he left home and ran wild at fourteen,
Drank homemade hooch from tin cans
And smoked Lucky's down to the tip,
Broke up country dancehalls just for fun.

Long before he went off to fight the Nazis.
He told the recruiter
If he saw Hitler over there
He'd kill him with his bare hands.
Even before he and my Mother eloped to Missouri
In the dark, in the rain,
His '38 Ford's headlights searching the night,
The back roads for love,
For the real thing,
As he used to say.

If I could only hear his voice one last time
Like Wisconsin granite underfoot.
His long arms good for fighting,
His strong working man's back that held up the world,
And his hands like catchers' mitts
That caught me and swept me up high into the air,
Carried me toward my future
And sat me down gently,
Then left me alone for good.

Dogs and P.O.W.'s

I

I remember how the dogs looked,
All dead and bound together in a wire cage,
Their lips still curled and snarling,
Caring even in death
That they would soon be someone's dinner,
Dragged down a dusty path
By a thousand year old woman
Gouging a trembling streak in the dust,
While we rode easily on behind her,
From Phuoc Le to Vung Tau,
Toward the silver beaches of the South China Sea,
Flattening it out all the way.

II

I remember they could squat forever
On the hard ground
Like they were part of it,
Only their lips moving
In their ancient tongue,
Chopped and giddy,
Like an interrupted song.
And they were patient, too.
They could hold onto an idea for hours
Or even longer,
Until I knew something
Like true love
Without understanding what it was.

Giving Blood

Phuong, which means Phoenix,
The twelve year old daughter of a friend
Who was once the enemy,
Had a tumor like a soccer ball
Growing within her.
So they trussed us up at the An Loc field hospital
Like deer for the slaughter
Punctured our arms with skinning knives,
Ran my blood into her vein through a clear plastic tube,
Like coral vine.

I dreamed filthy river water
Rose to her lips.
Red and white lotus floated around her.
She floundered,
Arms stiff like clubs at her sides,
Waiting for me to save her.

I dreamed my blood roiled through her veins,
Consumed her innocence,
Brought her down like
A rat in a snare trap,
Made her a whore and a killer.

I dreamed she ran toward me,
Her savior,
Fled from me,
Her enemy.

But she rose from the ashes
And lived to dance and to dream
Of future children,

Until her thirteenth birthday,
When a sniper bullet cracked her forehead
Like a rotten tomato.

She Said

I should just stop about the war,
She said.
The war happened long ago,
Like old dirt tire tracks
In an abandoned country road.
And I had to agree.
But it seems that I have nothing else
But the war
To talk about.

What Remains

I Thought I'd remember everything.
A Recorder of horror.
Camera Eyes.
Details.
Listen, I'd say.
This is what I saw.
This.
But now all that remains
Is a wiry old man naked to the waist
In a rocking sampan,
Pulling a rope for all he is worth,
Until the river swamps everything,
Everything.

Rick Christman's first book, *Falling in Love at the End of the World*, a collection of stories and prose poems, was published by New Rivers Press. His stories and poems have appeared in many magazines, including *Indiana Review, Connecticut Review, Wisconsin Review, Briar Cliff Review* and *Descant*. He is a winner of the Loft-McKnight Award in Fiction and the St. Louis Poetry Center's National Poetry Contest, judged by Stephen Dunn. *Searching for Mozart* is the 2014 winner of The Brighthorse Prize in Poetry. Until his retirement, Christman was Professor of Creative Writing and literature at Des Moines Area Community College in Iowa, where he was also the founder and director of the college's annual Celebration of the Literary Arts.

www.ingramcontent.com/pod-product-compliance
Lightning Source LLC
Chambersburg PA
CBHW021940040426
42448CB00008B/1164